Published in Atlanta, GA
by GamePlan Financial Marketing, LLC
ISBN: 978-0-615-87040-3

Designed by Katie DiGiovanna

800.886.4757
gameplanfinancial.com

1408098

A SIMPLE
PATH

5 STEPS TO HELP ENHANCE YOUR OVERALL FINANCIAL STRATEGIES

GAMEPLAN FINANCIAL MARKETING, LLC
Foreword by Ryan J. Perkins

The will to win is not nearly so important as the will to prepare to win.

—VINCE LOMBARDI

CONTENTS

FOREWORD i

INTRODUCTION 1

THREE GREAT CHALLENGES 13

STRAIGHTFORWARD STEP ONE 31
Diversify, Diversify, Diversify!

STRAIGHTFORWARD STEP TWO 39
Pass Go & Collect $200!

STRAIGHTFORWARD STEP THREE 45
Follow the Wisdom of the Gray Squirrel.

STRAIGHTFORWARD STEP FOUR 67
Fortify Your Income Stream.

STRAIGHTFORWARD STEP FIVE 89
Put Away Your Crystal Ball.

WHAT'S NEXT? 97

FOREWORD

" *If you always do what you have always done, you will always get what you have always gotten.*"

—MY HIGH SCHOOL BASKETBALL COACH

Of all of the times that I heard my high school coach say that, I never realized how profound that statement was, especially as it relates to personal finances.

If you're holding this book, chances are you are looking for an answer to the question *"How do I start planning for my retirement?"* Seeking new information is a great place to start. Are you up for a few challenges as you read along?

Challenge #1:
Read the book in its entirety and take notes.

When I joined the financial services industry, one of the first things I did was ask my parents, grand-parents, and other relatives about the questions that they have had with their financial situations. It amazed me how similar their questions were, regardless of age. The issues that consistently came up were things like:

■ *"Will I have enough money to retire on?*

- *"When should I plan to take my Social Security benefits?"*
- *"I'm concerned about the stock market's fluctuations. How can I prepare?"*
- *"How can I plan for inflation and taxes?"*

Because of their questions, I have developed a very simple personal philosophy as it relates to retirement income planning strategies:

1. Look to enhance your Social Security retirement benefits.
2. Look to increase income streams.
3. Seek to decrease income taxes, where possible.

In my opinion, if you do these things (in that order and with all three in mind), then you can improve the probability of achieving your retirement goals. This is a message that I am very passionate about. In fact, for the last several years, I have focused on educating financial professionals and their clients on concepts that help to prepare them for exactly this.

In my opinion, this book does a wonderful job of taking the first steps down the path. If you are anything like my family (and many others that I speak with across the country), you may have concerns about market fluctuations, inflation, and taxes... turning the page lets you begin to disarm these concerns.

Challenge #2:
Apply what you learn.

This book has tools designed to help you reach your financial retirement goals and dreams. Having knowledge of key fundamentals and then putting them into practice may be the most challenging, yet important part of the process.

To relate it back to my basketball days, the easy part for my coach was to get us to *want* to be better. The harder part was getting us to actually do the work and make the changes that it would take to make significant improvements.

After my freshman year, I told my coach that I wanted to dramatically improve my game and set myself up to be a great player on the varsity team. The first thing that he told me to do was to change my shooting. The problem for me was that I thought I was already a good shooter, and to think about changing that was a hard pill to swallow.

I worked all summer long on making that change, and yes, there were growing pains associated with that major change. In fact, my shooting percentage went down dramatically for the first two months. But by the time school had started, I had worked through the challenges and was seeing the results. Looking back, I must admit that the advice—as hard as it was to buy into and put into practice—was a key fundamental in my high school success and, more importantly, my preparation to play college basketball.

I tell you that story because your financial "game" can be very similar. If you read this book, you will get good basic guidance. But some of the tips might be tough to accept, just like when I first learned that I needed to change my shooting. However, if you are willing to apply some of the things you learn, you can set yourself up in a stronger position for your financial future. Your time is a huge investment, arguably the most important investment you could make. If you invest your time into reading this book, make sure there is a return on that investment. Apply what you learn, if appropriate, and there can be a payoff.

Challenge # 3:
Seek advice from a professional.

If you had a cavity in one of your teeth, what would you do?

Of course, it needs to be fixed. Where should you start? There are lots of books about dentistry out there. You could learn a lot about the mouth, teeth, cavities, fillings, and dentistry fundamentals.

But no matter how much you read or how much pain you were in, would you ever perform dental work on your own tooth?

Just like dentistry, preparing for retirement, in my opinion, is *not* a do-it-yourself adventure. The book that you are holding can set you on the path to making better choices for *you* and the specifics of your particular situation. No two individuals' financial needs are the same, and I'd encourage you to do the work to find the potentially optimal fit for you.

Wishing you all the best on your financial journey!

Ryan J. Perkins

INTRODUCTION

" *I need to retire from retirement.* "

—SANDRA DAY O'CONNOR

***Preparing for retirement
is not a simple task.***

Making decisions about your own retirement is a process of gathering information. We can't possibly outline all the decisions each individual will have to make in just one book. Our goal with this book, however, *is* simple.

Hopefully, when you finish this book, you will have:

- A basic understanding of some possible retirement strategies
- Helpful information to use in building out your own path to retirement
- Educated questions to ask your own financial professionals

THE RETIREMENT OF
YESTERDAY

"Old people love their own things even more than young people do. It means so much to sit in the same chair you sat in for a great many years."

—ELEANOR ROOSEVELT, 1934

1875

The American Express Company established the first private pension plan in the U.S.

1889

Over 100 years ago, the Germans created the old-age pension program, similar to the way that today's Social Security program works! It was financed by mandatory contributions from the worker, the employer, and the government. This pension paid benefits to workers who reached age 70.

1935

Franklin D. Roosevelt proposed the legislation that became the Social Security Act of 1935.

1946

1946 through 1964 marks the birth of the baby boomer generation. Beginning January 1, 2011, and for the next 19 years, every day, more than 10,000 baby boomers will reach the age of 65. *(That's one every 8.64 seconds.)*[1]

---

[1] *money.usnews.com, "The Baby Boomer Number Game," March 23, 2012.*

THE RETIREMENT OF
TODAY

" *The question isn't at what age
I want to retire, it's at what income.* "

—GEORGE FOREMAN

AGE 57

Tom plans to work as long as he can. *(One in three workers expect to retire at age 70 or never.)*

AGE 60

Dorothy and Warren, a couple both age 60, decided that they would like to continue to work in their present jobs until age 75 and then travel.

This hypothetical timeline is shown for illustrative purposes only.

AGE 62

Cindy will retire from her present job at age 62 and start her own business.

Whatever it is you choose to do, how can you prepare yourself for 20, 30, or even 40 years in retirement?

Turn the page.

THREE GREAT
CHALLENGES

When a man retires and time is no longer a matter of urgent importance, his colleagues generally present him with a watch.

—R. C. SHERRIFF

Hypothetical scenario:
Meet Jim and Mary.

Jim and Mary, like many baby boomers, have worked hard to prepare for their retirement. While raising three children (and sending all of them to college!), they also managed to save in Jim's 401(k) and have been planning for Jim's upcoming retirement. They're excited about the chance to travel, visit their grown children, and enjoy lots of leisure time together.

August 15: The big day

Jim dresses carefully for his last day in the office. While watching the news that morning, he barely notices the report that the housing market is starting to falter. Jim quietly enjoys his drive into the office, thinking of how many times he has driven this exact route.

The retirement party is fun—filled with cake, warm wishes, and promises to get together soon. That evening, Jim and Mary celebrate over dinner. It's the beginning of a beautiful thing.

Two years later...

It's been an interesting time. Though the stock market fluctuations have caused a drop in Jim's 401(k) value, both Jim and Mary are still feeling mostly confident about the reliability of Jim's pension and Social Security retirement benefits. More importantly, Jim has fished, golfed, and even "antiqued" to his (and Mary's) heart's content. In fact, he may be just the tiniest bit restless about spending so much time at "leisure."

Another two years go by...

Jim is relieved that his 401(k) balance has rebounded some after the recent market fluctuations, but Mary is concerned about how much more things cost. Their prescription drugs are more expensive, and even basic needs seem more expensive every year. Though their health is still good, health care costs have started to be more significant than they planned.

Three more years go by...
(Seven years into retirement)

Mary notices that Jim has been glued to the television. The President is delivering an address outlining the bill that was recently passed, which unfortunately raises taxes on millions of Americans, possibly including them. They are now concerned as to whether they can make it through retirement without going back to work. Frustrated, Jim and Mary begin to wonder where they went wrong in their retirement planning.

Jim and Mary did lots of things *right*. They've worked hard, diligently saved, and arrived at retirement with a pretty solid game plan. Unfortunately, their plan ran into Three Great Challenges of retirement:

- Market Fluctuations
- Inflation
- Taxes

Let's take a closer look.

MARKET FLUCTUATIONS

" October: This is one of the peculiarly dangerous months to speculate in stocks. The others are July, January, September, April, November, May, March, June, December, August, and February. "

—MARK TWAIN

The popular saying *"Buy low, sell high"* may be easier said than done, as many Americans discovered in some of the past downturns of the stock market. For retirees preparing to live off assets that they have accumulated, market fluctuations can be a possible game changer. Recovering from market losses takes time, and if you're approaching your planned retirement age, that may be the one thing you do *not* have.

Most pre-retirees are very interested in finding ways to stabilize their retirement savings and build a solid foundation of guaranteed income that they can live off of. This book has some key strategies like how fixed annuities can provide valuable income guarantees, for you to consider in making your retirement decisions.

One more quick question about market fluctuations: once you lose value, how hard is it to earn it back?

Hypothetical example: If you had retirement savings of $100,000 (a nice, easy round number) and lost 20% of it, how much would you have?

Original Value	$100,000
20% Loss	-$20,000
New Value	$80,000

Now to get *back* to $100,000, you'd need to re-earn $20,000, right? Remember, you have less money to earn growth from, so the $20,000 is a percentage of the new value of your account: $80,000.

And to earn $20,000, you'd need to get a 25% return on your $80,000.

Summary: When you lost 20%, you had to earn 25% to get back to the same starting place.

How can you protect your original principal and still supplement your retirement income? This book has some suggested strategies that may be able to help with your goals.

> In 2012, U.S. investors in their sixties have more than 48% of their 401(k) invested in equities.*

2014 Investment Company Fact Book, 54th edition, Investment Company Institute

Guarantees are backed by the financial strength and claims-paying ability of the issuing insurance company.

INFLATION

" Inflation is when you pay fifteen dollars for the ten-dollar haircut you used to get for five dollars when you had hair. "

—SAM EWING

We all know that over time, prices tend to go up…but how do you prepare for what could be a lengthy retirement?

Mary wasn't wrong when she noticed costs increasing just four years into retirement: the average price of milk in 2002 was $2.75, while the average price of milk in 2012 was $3.47.

Are you feeling the pinch?[1]

Take a look at just 10 years of change.

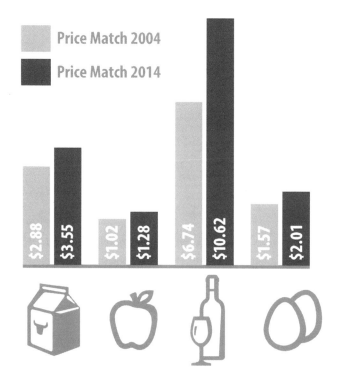

Price Match 2004
Price Match 2014

$2.88 $3.55 $1.02 $1.28 $6.74 $10.62 $1.57 $2.01

Did you know that Social Security retirement benefits are designed to be adjusted for inflation?

One of the most powerful components that Social Security has is what is known as **Cost of Living Adjustments (COLAs)**. These COLAs try to keep pace with inflation by possibly increasing your Social Security check each year.

The COLA that Social Security recipients received in 2014 was 1.5%, and for 2015, it is 1.7%.[2] Sometimes, people receiving Social Security benefits say that it doesn't feel like much of a "raise." However, you should remember this little feature as we will show you features that can imitate the COLA benefit later in this book.

---

[1]bls.gov, "Databases, Tables & Calculators by Subject," November 20, 2014.

[2]ssa.gov, "History Of Automatic Cost-Of-Living Adjustments," 2015.

CHALLENGE THREE
TAXES

" *The only difference between death and taxes is that death doesn't get worse every time Congress meets.* "

—WILL ROGERS

Average Tax Rates for the
Highest-Income Taxpayers, 1945–2009

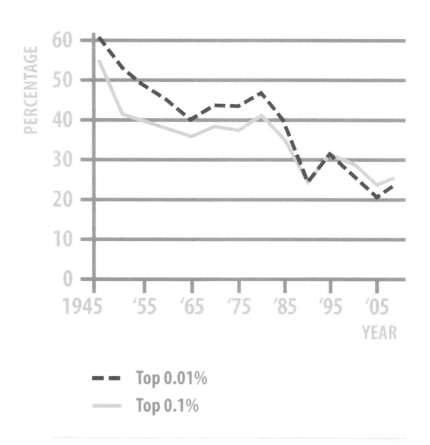

- - Top 0.01%
—— Top 0.1%

*Congressional Research Service, "Taxes and the
Economy: An Economic Analysis of the Top Tax
Rates Since 1945," December 12, 2012.*

Believe it or not, there is some good news for you about taxes. Historically speaking, *we are in a time of low tax rates.* It may not feel like low taxes, but check out the tax rates from the mid-1940s and the late 1970s.

As you know, budgeting for the United States government directly affects what we pay in taxes, and like any business, to get out of a deficit, the choices are to:

1. increase income and/or
2. decrease expenses.

We believe that the combination of our spiraling national debt and the relatively low income tax rates means we can expect taxes to increase over the next few decades.

More importantly, what do *you* think?

If you think taxes are headed:

Up

As you read the next section, the "Pay Now" strategy may make the most sense for you.

Down

As you read the next section, the "Pay Later" strategy may be the strongest option for you to consider.

Don't Know

Don't worry—lots of people are in this boat with you! Diversification can help keep plenty of options on the table for you.

Whichever option you just chose, this book will show strategies for you to consider. Can there be a straightforward path to plan for taxes in retirement? Absolutely.

Keep reading!

My Questions

☐ When would I like to retire? When can I afford to retire?

☐ How well have I prepared my retirement savings for market fluctuations, inflation, and income taxes?

☐ What Social Security benefits will I receive, and will those benefits and my current financial strategy be enough to support me when I retire?

Questions for My Financial Professional

☐ How will my Social Security benefits and my retirement assets be affected by market fluctuations, inflation, and income taxes? Do fixed annuities make sense for my financial situation?

☐ How can you help me reduce my tax liability in retirement?

[Continued]

[Continued]

Questions for My Financial Professional

☐ I'm interested in learning more about my Social
Security retirement benefits. Can you help me
with additional information or details on what
I might be able to expect?

Your Financial Professional can provide information, but not give tax or Social Security advice. You
should also seek guidance from your tax advisor
or the Social Security Administration regarding
your particular situation.

D^3

STRAIGHTFORWARD
STEP ONE

DIVERSIFY,
DIVERSIFY,
DIVERSIFY!

Diversification is a topic that is frequently discussed in the financial services world. In a nutshell, it's really as simple as this:

Don't put all your eggs in one basket. (Especially your nest egg!)

Often, diversification may be concerned with risk and asset classes. Those are important, but there's other kinds of diversification that may also be significant—tax diversification. It can help you to be prepared to respond to whatever may happen with taxes. One of the steps to help simplify your retirement planning is to consider tax diversification.

When it comes to paying income taxes, you really have three options:

- "Pay-As-You-Go" Basket
- "Pay Later" Basket
- "Pay Now" Basket

"Pay-As-You-Go" Basket

You're probably pretty familiar with some of the products in this group. They include things like stocks, mutual funds, savings accounts, and CDs. This basket comes with a Form 1099 each year, which is how you report any earnings from these financial products on your tax return. For these products, you literally pay income taxes as you earn money inside them.

"Pay Later" Basket

This group of products lets you be able to defer your income taxes. It includes things like 401(k)s, some annuities, and traditional IRAs. Assets within this tax classification grow tax-deferred, and ultimately, taxes are paid when the money is withdrawn.

"Pay Now" Basket

This group of products lets you pay taxes on your money *now*, enjoy income tax-free growth, and are currently designed to allow for income-tax free withdrawals. It includes items such as Roth IRAs, municipal bonds, and cash-value life insurance (CVLI).

"PAY-AS-YOU-GO"
BASKET

Remember:
Income taxes are paid yearly and are reported on your Form 1099.

Stocks

Mutual Funds

Savings Accounts

CDs

"PAY LATER"
BASKET

Remember:
Pay income taxes when the money is withdrawn.

401(k)s

Some Annuities

Traditional IRAs

"PAY NOW"
BASKET

Remember:
Pay taxes now, enjoy income tax-free growth, and access funds income tax-free.

Roth IRAs

Cash-Value Life Insurance (CVLI)*

Municipal Bonds

Income-tax free distributions are achieved by withdrawing to the cost basis (premiums paid), then using policy loans. Loans and withdrawals may generate an income tax liability, reduce available cash value and reduce the death benefit, or cause the policy to lapse. This assumes the policy qualifies as a life insurance and is not a modified endowment contract.

You may be thinking, *"Cash-value life insurance? I don't even know what that is!"*

You're probably most familiar with the death benefits of life insurance, which can be an awesomely powerful financial product. If life insurance is a right fit for you, there are other benefits and features that are available inside many of these policies. We'll go over these in more detail in **Straightforward Step Three.**

One more quick note...

As you're thinking over your own nest egg and which baskets it is currently in, there's something important to know about the "Pay Later" Basket. (As a reminder, this is the basket where you are contributing dollars that haven't been income-taxed yet. For most people, this basket contains their 401(k) and traditional IRAs.)

So what's the thing about this "Pay Later" Basket?

Well, it has a *countdown clock* attached to it. For money that is in this basket, the federal government is counting the years, months, and days until you turn 70½. At this precise age, the government will **require** you to start pulling money out each year in the form of required minimum distributions (RMDs).

The good news is that with proper planning, this doesn't have to be a hiccup in your plans.

Remember to always consult your tax advisor or attorney prior to making any decisions.

Summary: It may be wise to consider using all three baskets in your retirement planning strategy. Diversifying your nest egg from an income tax perspective leaves you with more options about where to build your income stream later.

If you're well tax diversified, you may be more prepared than Jim and Mary to respond to a changing tax environment.

This book is designed to provide general information on the subjects covered. It is not, however, intended to provide specific legal or tax advice and cannot be used to avoid tax penalties or to promote, market, or recommend any tax plan or arrangement. Please note that GamePlan Financial Marketing, LLC, its affiliated companies, and their representatives and employees do not give legal or tax advice. You are encouraged to consult your tax advisor or attorney.

My Questions

☐ On a scale of 1 to 10, how well diversified do I feel?

☐ Am I tax diversified?

☐ What is potentially the best strategy for me—paying taxes on my money now, later, or as I go?

Questions for My Financial Professional

☐ How can insurance products be used to help diversify my "buckets?"

☐ How can I incorporate tax-diversified products into my strategy?

☐ What role can Social Security/defined benefit (DB) plans play in my tax-diversification strategy?

STRAIGHTFORWARD
STEP TWO

PASS GO &
COLLECT $200!

Just like the classic board game, collecting "free money" is a simple step to enhance your retirement. What does that mean? If you currently have a 401(k) or 403(b) plan at work, you may also have a matching program. These matching contributions fall under the category of "free money" because they're given to you.* For this reason, you should consider contributing to your 401(k) or 403(b) in a way that lets you take full advantage of the matching program.

Other examples of "free money" would be gifts, inheritances, and winning the lottery. Without knowing details or timing, counting on these for your retirement plans might be a challenge. Let's focus on what you can control and let these other things be delightful surprises.

---

*Just like most programs, are there rules around when you can access the 401(k) matching contributions? Absolutely. Remember to consult with your employer's 401(k) plan sponsor with any questions that you may have.

**Hypothetical scenario:
Meet Mike.**

Mike is participating in his employer's 401(k) program. His company matches his 401(k) contributions dollar for dollar, up to 5% of his salary. (Nice match, isn't it?)

Mike is currently contributing 7% to his plan. When asked why he was contributing above the match, Mike explained that he wanted to capitalize on the "free money," and if 5% was good, then 7% must be even better!

Is Mike right? Well, kinda.

If you go back to the first paragraph of this step, you'll see that we strongly encouraged you to contribute to your 401(k) in a way that lets you take full advantage of your company's matching program. Once Mike contributes over and above the employer match percentage cap, he no longer recieves an employer provided benefit based on the additional contributions he chooses to make.

This really means that Mike needs to make a decision about that additional 2% that he's contributing—does he want to "Pay Later" or "Pay Now"? (Or even "Pay-As-You-Go" on his income taxes?)

He should consider other reasons beyond the employer match to determine if he wants to contribute above the match, or reallocate those contributions to other options.

As you may remember, 401(k) contributions are in the "Pay Later" Basket, which includes the rules about RMDs.* It may make sense to consider putting that money into a fixed annuity, which is also in the "Pay Later" Basket, or using the funds for a financial vehicle in the "Pay Now" Basket.

More info on required minimum distributions (RMDs) can be found on page 36.

That's not a typo—we really did mean that it might make sense to select a different product, even in the same "tax rule" basket. Why would you do that? Fixed annuities can offer some additional features that may be appealing, such as principal protection and a guaranteed stream of income.[1] If you're ready to learn more, you'll love **Straightforward Steps Four and Five!**

---

[1]*Guarantees are backed by the financial strength and claims-paying ability of the issuing insurance company. Any distributions may be subject to ordinary income tax and if taken prior to age 59½ an additional 10% federal tax.*

My Questions

☐ How much am I contributing to my 401(k) right now? What is my company match?

☐ Am I maximizing my potential for "free money" with a company match? If not, can I afford to contribute more?

☐ Am I taking advantage of ALL the benefit plans my employer offers?

Questions for My Financial Professional

☐ How can a fixed annuity offer me a guaranteed stream of income?

☐ What financial products can help me prepare for retirement after I meet my company match?

STRAIGHTFORWARD
STEP THREE

FOLLOW THE
WISDOM OF THE
GRAY SQUIRREL.

Have you ever watched a gray squirrel prepare for winter? Their strategy seems to include digging an enormous number of holes to hold their nuts for winter. Squirrels, as funny as it seems, could teach us a few things about the retirement planning process.

How?

- They tend to have a well-diversified nut portfolio, with stashes in a variety of locations.
- They have focused on preparation and have substantial stockpiles built to get them through the winter.
- They've worked to guard their stores against major threats (erosion, other animals, etc.).
- They may have even put away more than they need, knowing that some of the stores will be discovered.

Gray squirrels must be able to survive on the food stores that are both sufficiently protected and accessible—and your retirement savings are remarkably similar.

How?

Remember, it's not just about what you save and earn—it's about what you keep. Remember the section on the "Three Great Challenges" of retirement that we discussed? Taxes can eat a significant hole in your retirement savings, even beyond the threats of market fluctuations and inflation.

Taxes can nibble away at your nest egg—just like erosion, other animals, and losing acorns can make it challenging for squirrels to survive.

So what do you do? Consider ways to reduce your tax liability. Ready to learn more about how to do just this?

Keep reading!

"PAY-AS-YOU-GO"
BASKET

Remember:
Income taxes are paid yearly and are reported on your Form 1099.

Stocks
Mutual Funds
Savings Accounts
CDs

"PAY LATER"
BASKET

Remember:
Pay income taxes when the money is withdrawn.

401(k)s
Some Annuities
Traditional IRAs

"PAY NOW"
BASKET

Remember:
Pay taxes now, enjoy income tax-free growth, and access funds income tax-free.

Roth IRAs
Cash-Value Life Insurance (CVLI)*
Municipal Bonds

* Income-tax free distributions are achieved by withdrawing to the cost basis (premiums paid), then using policy loans. Loans and withdrawals may generate an income tax liability, reduce available cash value and reduce the death benefit, or cause the policy to lapse. This assumes the policy qualifies as a life insurance and is not a modified endowment contract.

48

MUNICIPAL BONDS

" *I'm proud to be paying taxes in the United States. The only thing is, I could be just as proud for half the money.* "

—ARTHUR GODFREY

What are they?

Municipal bonds are bonds that have been issued by a government (usually a city or a state) that gets a special kind of tax treatment. Typically, municipal bonds have been seen as a conservative investment option that is primarily attractive because the earnings are tax-exempt.*

What are the additional things to consider?

- Are the current interest rates sufficient to keep pace with inflation?
- How diversified is this option? (Remember **Straightforward Step One: Diversify, Diversify, Diversify!**)
- The overall risk of this choice. What are the default rates on municipal bonds?
- What kind of effect could this income have on my Social Security benefits?

Some municipal bonds are not tax-exempt. Work with an appropriately registered financial services professional who is currently affiliated with a properly registered broker/dealer or a registered investment advisor to get your questions answered.

Including municipal bonds in your retirement strategy may make sense, especially if you're building a stream of tax-free income in retirement. Working with a financial services professional that is currently affiliated with a properly registered broker/dealer or a registered investment advisor can help you find the right balance of this product in your overall plan.

ROTH IRAs

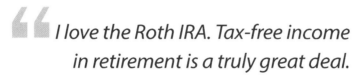

I love the Roth IRA. Tax-free income in retirement is a truly great deal.

—SUZE ORMAN

What are they?

Roth IRAs are funded with money that has already been taxed, such as your "take-home" earnings or money from your savings account. Roth IRAs are extremely popular options because the money inside them grows income tax-free and generally is withdrawn income tax-free.

There are certain circumstances in which Roth IRA distributions can be taxable because there are taxable situations. Please work with a tax professional and a broker/dealer or investment advisor representative to make the best choices for you.

Roth IRA earnings can be withdrawn income tax-free as long as you are age 591/2 or older and have owned the IRA for at least five years. That five-year clock starts on January 1 of the tax year in which you make your initial Roth IRA contribution. For a more detailed discussion of the calculation of a qualified distribution from a Roth IRA, please see your preferred tax professional.

What are some additional things to consider?

Some may say that the Roth IRA's drawback is only that the federal government limits how much money you can contribute to it each year.

As of 2013, the maximum amount that can be contributed to a Roth IRA, in one calendar year, is $5,500 per individual. There's a couple of additional rules that go with that:

1. If you're over age 50, you are allowed to contribute an additional $1,000 per year per person.

2. For married couples, if your modified adjusted gross income (MAGI)[1] is more than $188,000, you cannot contribute at all.

---

[1] Modified adjusted gross income includes reportable income increased by certain tax-exempt amounts, such as tax-exempt interest, exclusions for qualified U.S. savings bonds interest, adoption benefits, foreign earned income or housing, and allowable IRA deduction.

Here are additional guidelines for other filing statuses and income levels that may cause a phaseout of the allowed contribution for you to bear in mind. Again, working with a tax professional on the specifics of your situation is important!

Let's look at some hypothetical examples:

Bob and Martha, age 57 and 59, respectively, want to contribute to a Roth IRA. Their MAGI is $85,000.

> **Q1:** How much can they contribute?_____
>
> **Q2:** If their MAGI was $192,000, how much could they contribute?_____
>
> **Q3:** If Bob and Martha were age 42 and 44, respectively, and their MAGI was $85,000, how much could they contribute?_____

Answers can be found on page 59.

How do you get one?

- Open a new Roth IRA account with a qualified financial institution and deposit money that has already been subject to income tax.

- In some situations, it may make sense to convert a traditional IRA to a Roth IRA. Please note that a Roth conversion is a taxable event in the year of the conversion; therefore, this can have a substantial consequence on your personal tax situation, including, but not limited to, the taxation of current Social Security benefits.

It is generally preferable that you have funds to pay the income taxes due upon conversion from funds outside of your IRA. If you elect to take a distribution from your IRA to pay the conversion taxes, please keep in mind the potential consequences, such as an assessment of product surrender charges or additional IRS penalties for premature distributions.

You should *definitely* talk to a professional before you decide to do this!

This book is designed to provide general information on the subjects covered. Pursuant to IRS Circular 230, it is not, however, intended to provide specific legal or tax advice and cannot be used to avoid tax penalties or to promote, market, or recommend any tax plan or arrangement. Please note that GamePlan Financial Marketing, LLC, its affiliated companies, and their representatives and employees do not give legal or tax advice. You are encouraged to consult your tax advisor or attorney.

A1: **$13,000** ($5,500 for each of them, plus $1,000 catch-up contributions for each as they are both over the age of 50.)

A2: **$0** (They've hit the earnings threshold and cannot contribute.)

A3: **$11,000** ($5,500 for each of them.)

CASH-VALUE LIFE INSURANCE (CVLI)

>   *Retirement is like a long vacation in Las Vegas. The goal is to enjoy it to the fullest, but not so fully that you run out of money.*

—JONATHAN CLEMENTS

Any discussion of life insurance will always start with the death benefit. This product is a powerful option to help ensure that your loved ones are financially cared for, even after you're gone. But some of today's life insurance products have additional features that you should know about, which can be useful as you plan for your retirement years.

Specifically, this refers to cash-value life insurance (CVLI). These policies are designed to provide a death benefit over the course of your lifetime and also allow for cash value to build up inside. Because of some tax treatment rules, a properly designed and funded CVLI policy can provide a supplemental source of funds that is accessible via an income tax-free policy loan in your retirement years.

Yes, you read that correctly. CVLI policies can provide cash value accumulation potential. Available cash value may be accessed, via policy loans or withdrawals to assist with some financial goals, such as supplemental funds in retirement. From a taxation perspective, it works very much like a Roth IRA does, but without the contribution limitations that Roth IRAs have.

Are there rules about funding a CVLI policy?

Absolutely. You'll notice that we said that the policy has to be "properly designed and funded." Working with an appropriately licensed financial services professional and your tax advisor is SUPER important in making sure that this is set up correctly.

CVLI has three substantial benefits:

1. Just like the other options in the "Pay Now" Basket, CVLI grows tax-deferred.

2. You can access the built-up cash value inside the life insurance policy through contractually guaranteed provisions that allow you to receive the money income tax-free.

3. If structured properly, there is a death benefit that can be paid out to your beneficiaries without being subject to income taxes. This death benefit can still be available to your beneficiaries even once you have taken cash value out of your policy. However, be aware that if you pull cash value from your policy, the death benefit may be reduced.

Keep in mind that most life insurance policies require health underwriting and, in some cases, financial underwriting. It is also important to note that policy loans and withdrawals will reduce available cash values and death benefits and may cause the policy to lapse or affect any guarantees against lapse. Additional premium payments may be required to keep the policy in force. In the event of a lapse, outstanding policy loans in excess of unrecovered cost basis will be subject to ordinary income tax. And of course, tax laws are subject to change.

Whether you choose municipal bonds, Roth IRAs, CVLI, or a custom blend of all three, looking at ways to reduce your tax liability can be an important step in your path to retirement.

The rules governing the taxation of death benefits can be complicated—please work with an appropriately licensed financial services professional and a tax professional for details.

My Questions

☐ How well protected is my nest egg from outside forces? Do I want more protection?

☐ How well did my current investments do last year?

☐ How can I diversify my portfolio more? Where is my money going now, and what are the risks?

Questions for My Financial Professional

☐ Are there income tax-free options I should consider adding to my retirement planning strategies?

☐ Are there any limits to what I can contribute to the different retirement products you recommend?

STRAIGHTFORWARD
STEP FOUR

FORTIFY YOUR
INCOME STREAM.

A recent study on retirement included this conclusion: Americans fear outliving their money more than they fear death.[1] We think that fear is pretty understandable—if you outlive your money, where would you live? How would you eat? Would you have to move in with your family? Losing your independence can be a scary proposition.

How can you help keep that from happening?

We recommend having a game plan. Working with a financial services professional can help make this process less difficult.

---

[1] *Allianz Life Insurance Company of North America (Allianz), "Reclaiming the Future," Five Financial Personalities White Paper, 2013.*

How can you help ensure that you have a comfortable stream of income in retirement? Let's look at how retirement income has traditionally been built. Here are the three major columns of retirement income sources:

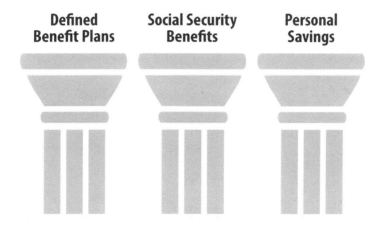

Defined Benefit Plans   **Social Security Benefits**   **Personal Savings**

DEFINED BENEFIT PLANS

" *I'm not just retiring from the company, I'm also retiring from my stress, my commute, my alarm clock, and my iron.* "

—HARTMAN JULE

Generally, when people are asked how they feel about having a defined benefit (DB) plan, they are almost always ravingly enthusiastic in their response. A DB plan, such as a pension, is usually very popular with participants because it provides a source of income **for the rest of their lives, guaranteed.*** Unfortunately, we're seeing less and less of these being offered by employers.

For example: In 1979, of employees with a retirement plan at work, less than 33% of private sector workers were covered by a DB plan; by 2011, that number dropped to just 3%.[1]

**Guarantees are backed by the financial strength and claims-paying ability of the issuer.*

[1]*Employee Benefit Research Institute: Fast Facts, March 28, 2013.*

True story: In 2006, Delta Airlines announced that it was terminating its pilot pension program, leaving 6,000 pilots "up in the air" about what they could expect in retirement. Though a governmental agency stepped in to help rescue the plan, ultimately, the participants ended up with reduced benefits as they headed into their retirement years.

Ouch! For someone trying to build a strong retirement income stream, a DB plan can be incredibly valuable. What do you do if you're part of the majority of Americans that don't have a DB plan?

Keep reading...

SUPPORT COLUMN TWO

SOCIAL SECURITY BENEFITS

" Retirement at sixty-five is ridiculous. When I was sixty-five I still had pimples.

"

—GEORGE BURNS

Retirement benefits from Social Security have taken on an enormously important role in retirement planning for Americans. Some might argue that these benefits are relied on FAR more than the system is designed to support.

How much are these benefits being utilized?

- 90% of Americans age 65 and older receive Social Security retirement benefits.[1]
- For 22% of married couples and 47% of unmarried persons, it is 90% or more of their income.[1]
- For workers with average earnings, Social Security benefits end up replacing close to 40% of their pre-retirement income.[2]

[1]ssa.gov, "Social Security Basic Facts," April 2, 2014.
[2]ssa.gov, "Understanding the Benefits," January 2014.

If nothing changes, the Social Security Trust Funds are projected to be depleted by 2033, according to the 2013 Social Security Trustees Report. Will we see changes to help plump up the reserve account? Some people may believe that there's no way to avoid it. Some people may also believe that eliminating the one thing that Americans have relied on as their base retirement income source is highly unlikely.

What makes Social Security so popular? Three things:

1. A source of income for the rest of your life, **_guaranteed._**

2. Cost of Living Adjustments (COLAs), which can help your income keep pace with inflation.

3. Your benefits can be provided to your family, in case you're not there to help support them.

What does this mean for you? Getting a better picture of what you can expect from Social Security is more important than ever. SSA.gov is a great resource for information on Social Security. In addition, your financial professional may be able to review different filing options available for your situation. Your financial professional can help you identify any retirement income gaps where an insurance product, such as a fixed annuity, may be of value. Working with a financial services professional can help you get answers to these important questions.

Did you know? There are multiple filing strategies that can be used to enhance your Social Security retirement benefits.

SUPPORT COLUMN THREE
PERSONAL SAVINGS

" You can retire from a job, but don't ever retire from making extremely meaningful contributions in life. "

—STEPHEN COVEY

This column is made up of a number of items that we've discussed already—mutual funds, stocks, 401(k)s, IRAs, and actual savings accounts. This area is the part of your retirement strategy that you have the most control of and is a place where you can most easily fortify your income stream. How can we use personal savings assets to re-create the benefits that can be enjoyed in the first two columns? Well, you can:

1. Create a source of income for the rest of your life, *guaranteed with the use of fixed annuities.** (Similar to a DB plan [or pension] and Social Security retirement benefits)

2. Possibly replicate the increases found in COLA's via optional, add-on riders to some annuity products. This can help your income address inflation concerns. (Similar to Social Security retirement benefits)

Guarantees are backed by the financial strength and claims-paying ability of the issuing insurance company.

3. Help ensure that your retirement savings are provided to your family, in case you're not there to help support them.

There are insurance products available that can do exactly those things. Regardless of how you choose to build your nest egg, these products can help transform it into a guaranteed stream of income for life, with the possibility of increases and a death benefit to be paid to your family.

There are various types of annuities, but we are going to discuss one popular type.

Fixed index annuities (FIAs).

How do they work?

A fixed index annuity (FIA) can provide principal protection, the potential for tax-deferred growth, a death benefit for your beneficiaries, and several income options. In addition, an FIA has the potential to earn interest based on changes in an external index.[1]

FIAs are designed to meet retirement and other long-term goals for a portion of your retirement savings. They are not suitable for meeting short-term goals because substantial surrender charges may apply if you surrender the contract before the end of the contract surrender period.

---

[1]*Although an external index or indices may affect contract values, the contract does not directly participate in any stock or equity investments. Consumers are not buying shares of any stock or index.*

Hypothetical scenario:
Let's meet Sarah.

Sarah is a healthy 58-year-old, currently earning $100,000 a year. Her retirement plans include watching the running of the bulls in Spain, driving the autobahn in Germany, and riding a camel across Egypt. She has done some preliminary budget planning for retirement and thinks that she will need $50,000 per year in retirement to support her lifestyle.

In saving for retirement, she accumulated $500,000 in a 401(k) that she rolled into an IRA 10 years ago.

She recently sat down with her financial professional to look at her possible options for Social Security benefits. Though she could file for benefits at age 62, she made the decision to wait until her full retirement age of 66 to file for her Social Security retirement benefits.

Let's look at her retirement budget once she is age 66:

Income Needed	$50,000 / yr
DB Plan	—
Social Security Benefits	$32,502 / yr
Needed from Savings	$17,498

Q: What can she do to cover those expenses? She can, of course, pull the money out of her IRA, as needed. (How long can she live off that money? How can she be SURE she doesn't outlive her money?)

A: She can also transfer a portion of her funds from her $500,000 IRA into an FIA with an optional income rider available at an additional cost. Fixed annuities have long been able to provide a lifetime stream of income through annuitization. Purchasing an optional income rider can provide some additional features, such as the opportunity for increasing income, which can help reduce inflation risk.

Sarah and her financial professional are careful to choose a product that also allows for a potential increase in income each year and pays out a death benefit when she passes away.* The projected income that is generated helps fill the income gap, and Sarah knows that she has a strong foundation of guaranteed income to get her through her retirement years.

Not all product features are available on all products. For full details on fixed index annuities, income riders, optional features, and associated costs, please work with an insurance-licensed financial services professional.

Guarantees are backed by the financial strength and claims-paying ability of the issuing insurance company.

Best of all, because she now has fortified her retirement income, she feels more comfortable in using some of her savings to travel the way she's always wanted to.

Is Sarah's answer right for everyone? Nope. Understanding the options that are available and learning from other people's decisions can be helpful. If you're ready to find a possible strategy for you, then call or e-mail the financial professional that gave you this book. It's a great place to get started.

Recreating the three columns of support can be challenging in today's environment. No matter where you are in the process of building your game plan, it may make sense to let a professional take a look. And now you know what to ask!

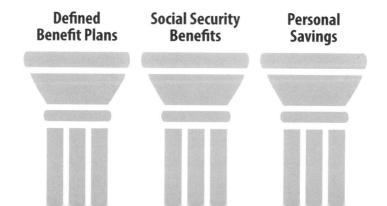

| Defined Benefit Plans | Social Security Benefits | Personal Savings |

My Questions

☐ How much retirement income will I need, and am I facing income gaps?

☐ Should I consider fortifying my income stream through the use of an FIA?

☐ Should I consider a CVLI policy to help supplement income needed in retirement?

Questions for My Financial Professional

☐ What are the pros and cons of fixed annuities, and how do I determine if I should add them to my retirement strategy?

☐ Do you have information about the different Social Security benefits filing strategies?*

☐ Should I consider CVLI as well to help supplement funds needed in retirement?

It's important to note that financial professionals are not endorsed by US government or any governmental agency. We encourage you to reach out to the Social Security Administration or www.ssa.gov for questions and information on Social Security.

STRAIGHTFORWARD
STEP FIVE

PUT AWAY YOUR
CRYSTAL BALL.

All too often, making retirement planning decisions requires guessing about where the stock market, interest rates, T-bill rates, etc. are going to go. Finding a way to maximize the *upside* of your options and minimize the *downside* risk can be exhausting. Isn't there any sort of "cruise control" that you can use?

There sure is.

As previously mentioned, some products, such as FIAs, allow you to accumulate interest based on a chosen market index (with a cap) and eliminate market fluctuation risk. What you may not have known is that the same indexing features exist inside life insurance policies.

Here's an example,
using a hypothetical market index.

If there's one thing that perhaps everyone can agree on, it's that the market will go up and the market will go down, right? It might look like this:

Hypothetical Market Index

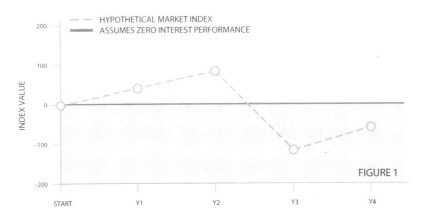

FIGURE 1

What if you could have your financial results look more like *this?*

Hypothetical Market Index

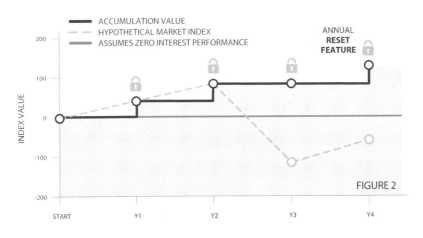

FIGURE 2

91

With the purchase of any additional-cost riders, the contract's values will be reduced by the cost of the rider. This may result in a reduction of your principal in any year in which the contract does not earn interest or earns interest in an amount less than the rider charge. This illustration does not take into surrender charges, which may apply to early withdrawals.

This hypothetical market index is provided for illustrative purposes only, using one type of interest calculation method. It is not intended to represent the performance of any specific product. No one crediting method credits the most interest in all market scenarios.

Actual results would be subject to caps, spreads, participation rates, or other limiting factors.

Although an external index or indices may affect contract values, the contract/policy does not directly participate in any stock or equity investments. You are not buying shares of any stock or index.

In Figure 3 below, the solid line reflects your policy values growing with the market, up to a capped value. It also shows your policy values *locked in* and not decreasing in value when the market index declines.

The arrow shows you an example of where your policy or contract values start to grow again, even though the market index is still down from its original value. And here's the exciting part about annual reset: in the hypothetical example below, you don't have to regain all the value that you would have lost in order to see growth.

Hypothetical Market Index

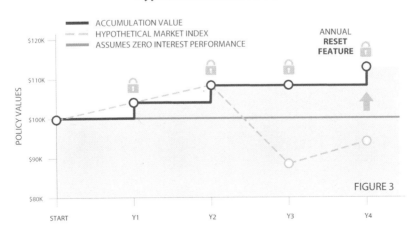

FIGURE 3

This product feature is known as "annual reset" and is available inside products that are "indexed."

The next question is simple—which line would you rather have?

If it's the one that can help protect you from market fluctuations, then see your preferred financial services professional today to let them know how they can help you. Understanding how various financial vehicles can work for *you* can help you feel confident in your retirement strategy.

My Questions

☐ Are there options for my retirement assets that don't include market risk?

☐ Should I protect a portion of my income from market downturns?

Questions for My Financial Professional

☐ Do fixed index products really guarantee no money loss due to market fluctuations? How do surrenders and/or withdrawals work?

☐ Is there a limit on earning potential and growth with fixed index products?

☐ How can I take advantage of "annual reset," how does it work, and what types of products allow it?

Guarantees are backed by the financial strength and claims-paying ability of the issuing insurance company.

WHAT'S NEXT?

> *Rule #1: Never lose money.*
> *Rule #2: Never forget rule #1.*

—WARREN BUFFETT

STRAIGHTFORWARD STEP ONE
Diversify, Diversify, Diversify!

STRAIGHTFORWARD STEP TWO
Pass Go & Collect $200!

STRAIGHTFORWARD STEP THREE
Follow the Wisdom of the Gray Squirrel.

STRAIGHTFORWARD STEP FOUR
Fortify Your Income Stream.

STRAIGHTFORWARD STEP FIVE
Put Away Your Crystal Ball.

WHAT'S NEXT?

If you are one of the many of Americans who don't feel prepared for retirement, now's a great time to start building your game plan. Here's what you can do:

1. Take a look at your anticipated Social Security benefits. Work with the insurance professional that gave you this book to get a personalized assessment of some filing options that may make sense for you and help you identify any retirement income gaps where an insurance product may be a good solution.

2. Roll up your sleeves and take a good, hard look at your finances. However far along you are, talking with insurance professionals, advisors and qualified tax and legal professionals can help! Make an appointment and sit down to discuss options.

3. Have a plan! With the five straightforward steps in this book, we hope you have a *path* to be able to help you build the retirement you desire.